EXPLORING OUR SOLAR SYSTEM

GAS GIANTS

HUGE FAR OFF WORLDS

DAVID JEFFERIS

Crabtree Publishing Company
www.crabtreebooks.com

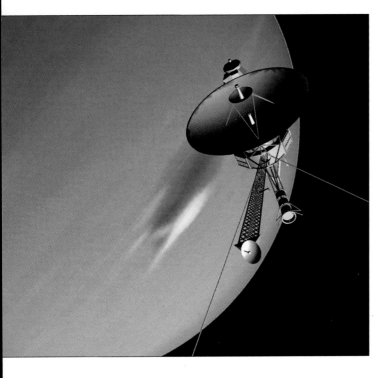

■THE GAS GIANTS

There are four huge "**gas giant**" planets in our **solar system**. Jupiter and Saturn are the biggest, but this book is about the other two, Uranus and Neptune. These are the planets furthest from the Sun, **orbiting** in the outer limits of the solar system.

Uranus and Neptune have little in common with Earth. Unlike our warm planet, they are dark, ultra-cold places. The Sun is so far away that it provides little heat or light. You could not walk on these planets either. They have no solid surface at all, and are just endless bands of clouds.

Crabtree Publishing Company

PMB 16A,
350 Fifth Avenue, Suite 3308
New York, NY 10118

616 Welland Avenue,
St. Catharines, Ontario
L2M 5V6

Published by Crabtree
Publishing Company
© 2009

Written and produced by:
David Jefferis/Buzz Books
Educational advisor:
Julie Stapleton
Science advisor:
Mat Irvine FBIS
Editor: Ellen Rodger
Copy editor:
Adrianna Morganelli
Proofreader: Crystal Sikkens
Project editor: Robert Walker
Production coordinator:
Katherine Kantor

■ ACKNOWLEDGEMENTS
We wish to thank all those people who have helped to create this publication. Information and images were supplied by:

Agencies and organizations:
ESA European Space Agency
Hubble images: STSci
JPL Jet Propulsion Laboratory
NASA National Aeronautics and Space Administration
Stellarium/Sourceforge
The Boeing Company
W.M. Keck Observatory

Collections and individuals:
Alpha Archive
Donald E. Davis
Calvin J. Hamilton
Jack Higgins/The Celestia Motherlode
David Jefferis
Visual of Galatea, courtesy J.I. Fish

Library and Archives Canada Cataloguing in Publication

Jefferis, David
Gas giants : huge far off worlds / David Jefferis.

(Exploring our solar system)
Includes index.
ISBN 978-0-7787-3734-6 (bound).--ISBN 978-0-7787-3750-6 (pbk.)

1. Uranus (Planet)--Juvenile literature. 2. Neptune (Planet)--Juvenile literature. I. Title. II. Series: Exploring our solar system (St. Catharines, Ont.)

QB681.J43 2008   j523.47   C2008-903638-7

Library of Congress Cataloging-in-Publication Data

Jefferis, David.
Gas giants : huge far off worlds / David Jefferis.
p. cm. -- (Exploring our solar system)
Includes index.
ISBN-13: 978-0-7787-3750-6 (pbk. : alk. paper)
ISBN-10: 0-7787-3750-0 (pbk. : alk. paper)
ISBN-13: 978-0-7787-3734-6 (reinforced library binding : alk. paper)
ISBN-10: 0-7787-3734-9 (reinforced library binding : alk. paper)
1. Uranus (Planet)--Juvenile literature. 2. Neptune (Planet)--Juvenile literature. I. Title. II. Series.

QB681.J44 2009
523.4--dc22

2008025374

6/11 Donation [26.65]

CONTENTS

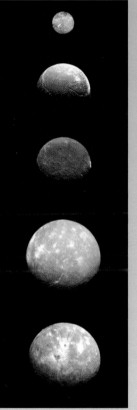

■WHAT ARE GAS GIANTS?

They are the four biggest planets in the solar system. Of these, Uranus and Neptune are the two planets furthest from the Sun.

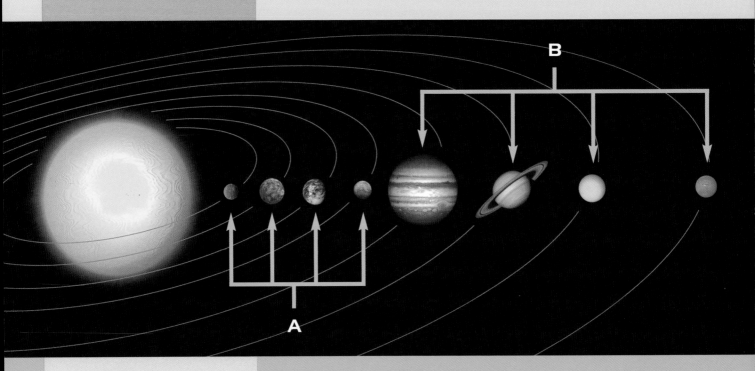

B

A

■ **Four planets (A) are closest to the Sun. From left to right, they are – Mercury, Venus, Earth, Mars. Beyond are the gas giants (B) – Jupiter, Saturn, Uranus, Neptune.**

■ HOW BIG ARE URANUS AND NEPTUNE?

Compared with the Earth, they are BIG! Uranus is about four times wider, at 31,765 miles (51,120 km) across. Neptune is a little smaller, at 30,775 miles (49,528 km). Even so, they are both dwarfed by the other gas giants, Jupiter and Saturn.

■ HOW FAR AWAY FROM THE SUN ARE THEY?

Uranus circles the Sun about 1,787 million miles (2,876 million km) away, and Neptune 2,829 million miles (4,553 million km). These distances are enormous, so astronomers usually use **Astronomical Units (AU)** instead. One AU is Earth's average distance from the Sun, or about 93 million miles (150 million km). On this easy-to-use scale, Uranus is 19.2 AU out, and Neptune is a far-off 30.1 AU.

WOW!
Each planet moves around the Sun in a near-circular path, called its orbit. The many moons in the solar system move in far smaller orbits, around their parent planets.

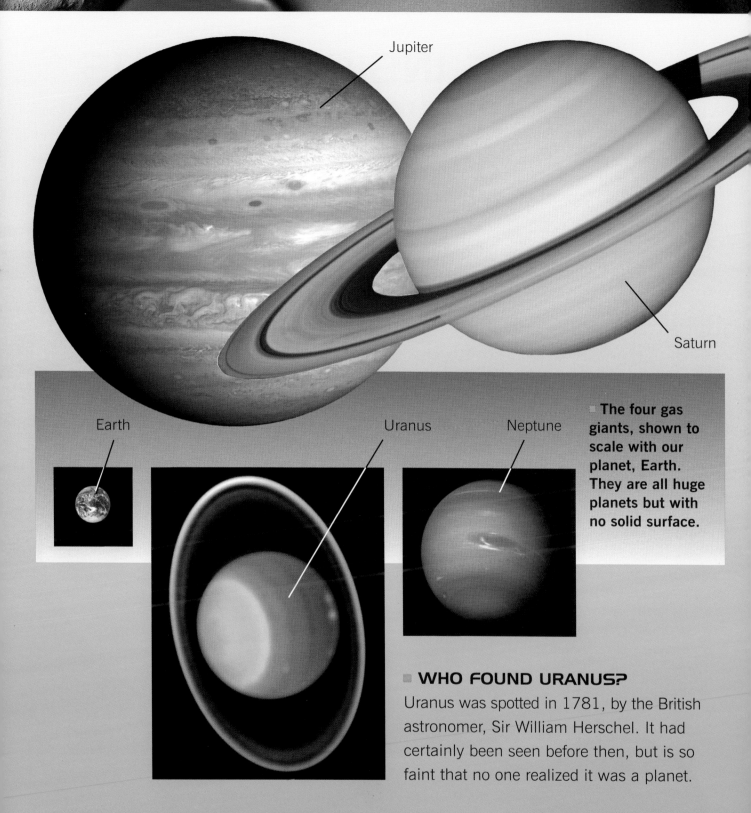

Jupiter

Saturn

Earth

Uranus

Neptune

The four gas giants, shown to scale with our planet, Earth. They are all huge planets but with no solid surface.

WHO FOUND URANUS?

Uranus was spotted in 1781, by the British astronomer, Sir William Herschel. It had certainly been seen before then, but is so faint that no one realized it was a planet.

HOW WAS NEPTUNE FIRST DISCOVERED?

Neptune was found in 1846, through the work of French mathematician Urbain Le Verrier. He knew that the motion of Uranus was affected slightly by a mystery space object – Neptune – and he calculated exactly where it could be seen with a telescope!

■WHAT'S INSIDE URANUS AND NEPTUNE?

They are made mostly of the gases hydrogen **and** helium, **plus other substances such as water,** methane **and** ammonia.

■ This is what scientists think lies inside Uranus.

At the very center of the planet is its core **(1)**, which may be as hot as 8,500°F (4,700°C).

The core is surrounded by the cooler mantle **(2)**, a mixture of ammonia, methane, and water.

The lower atmosphere **(3)** comes next. This consists of gases such as hydrogen, helium, and methane.

The upper atmosphere **(4)** finishes with the cloud tops that we can see with telescopes and cameras.

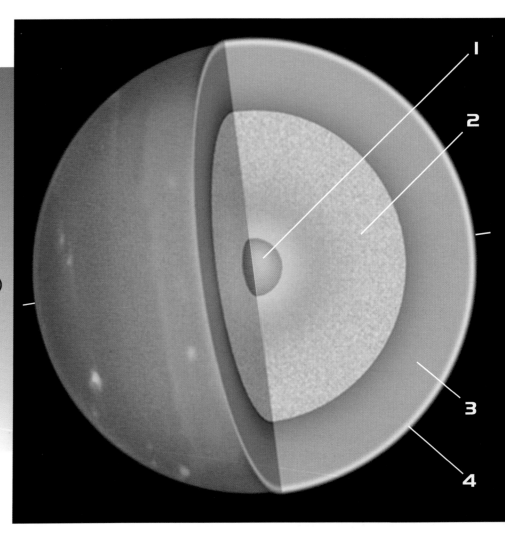

WOW!
Both planets orbit far from the Sun, so their "year" is very long. Uranus takes 84.3 Earth-years to complete an orbit, Neptune is even longer, at 164.8 years.

■ WHY ARE THEY ALSO KNOWN AS "ICE GIANTS"?

Like the bigger gas giants Jupiter and Saturn, Uranus and Neptune are made up mostly of hydrogen and helium. They also contain **"ices,"** substances such as water, ammonia, and methane. These "ices" are not like ice cubes or snowflakes. The term "ice" is used by astronomers to describe volatiles, or substances with low boiling points.

■ The solar system probably looked much like this about 4.6 billion years ago. Planets that formed near the Sun were small and rocky. Those that formed further away became the four gas giants.

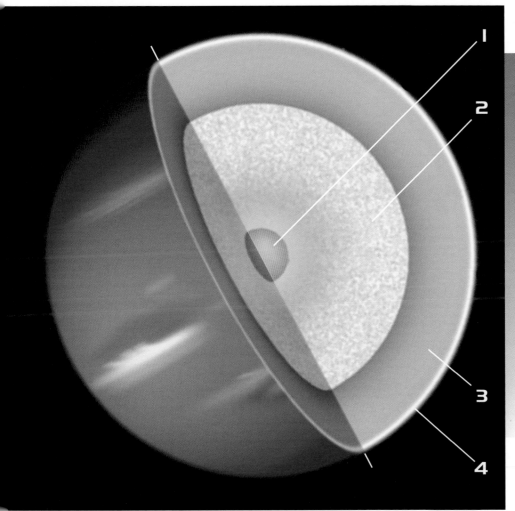

I
2
3
4

■ Neptune's makeup is similar to Uranus, although the core (1) is even hotter. The mantle (2) is thought to be about 4,000°F (2,200°C).

Heat passes through the lower and upper atmosphere (3, 4). But the cloud-tops are a chilly -330°F (-201°C).

■ Planet Earth, shown below to scale, has a very different interior. The core is thought to be molten iron and nickel, while the mantle is molten rock within a few miles of the solid surface.

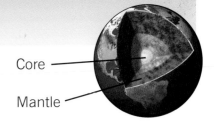

Core

Mantle

■ HOW OLD ARE THEY?

Like the Sun and other planets, they are thought to have formed from a huge disk of dust and rock about 4.6 billion years ago. It is believed that they were not big enough to attract as many gases as Jupiter and Saturn.

■ ARE THEY VERY COLD?

They are the furthest planets from the Sun, so not surprisingly, they are incredibly cold places. The chilliest atmosphere belongs to Uranus. Neptune, the furthest planet from the Sun, is actually a little warmer!

■HOW DO WE KNOW ABOUT THESE PLANETS?

A lot of information came from the 1980s Voyager 2 space probe. Today, the Hubble Space telescope (HST) is used, as are ground-based telescopes.

■ WHEN WAS VOYAGER'S MISSION?

Voyager 2 was one of a pair of probes sent to explore Jupiter and Saturn in the 1980s. After passing these planets, Voyager 2 went on to fly by Uranus in 1986, and Neptune in 1989.

■ Until Voyager 2's flight past Uranus, we could see its moons only as pinpricks of light. The probe sent back close-ups, such as this picture of the moon Ariel. It also spotted 10 moons that had been unknown until then.

■ WHERE IS VOYAGER NOW?

Voyager 2 and Voyager 1 are both far beyond the planets. Voyager 1 is furthest, at more than 100 AU from the Sun. Both space probes are still in working order, despite having been launched back in 1977. They are studying deep space as they go.

WOW!
Voyager 2 passed within 50,600 miles (81,500 km) of Uranus. It sounds like a lot until you think how far the probe had traveled. It is a great navigator.

■ WHAT ABOUT THE HST'S IMAGES?

Nothing compares with Voyager 2's close-ups. The Hubble Space Telescope does take a lot of useful pictures. Most importantly, the HST allows astronomers to get a long-term idea of what's happening on the gas giants, especially how storms in their atmospheres grow and fade over time.

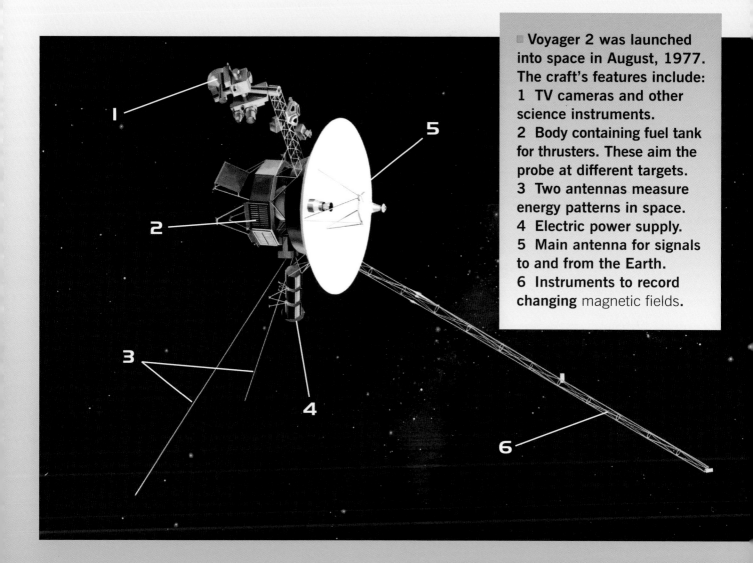

Voyager 2 was launched into space in August, 1977. The craft's features include:
1 TV cameras and other science instruments.
2 Body containing fuel tank for thrusters. These aim the probe at different targets.
3 Two antennas measure energy patterns in space.
4 Electric power supply.
5 Main antenna for signals to and from the Earth.
6 Instruments to record changing magnetic fields.

HOW USEFUL ARE GROUND-BASED TELESCOPES?

Like the HST, telescopes such as those at the Keck Observatory on Hawaii, can be used for long periods. The latest computer-aided equipment means that these instruments give much better results than in the past.

The HST orbits in space, high above the Earth. This allows it to have a clear view of space objects, free of blurriness caused by bad weather, or shifting air patterns in the atmosphere. The 11-ton (10 tonne) telescope has been in space since 1990, and still gives amazing pictures of objects in space.

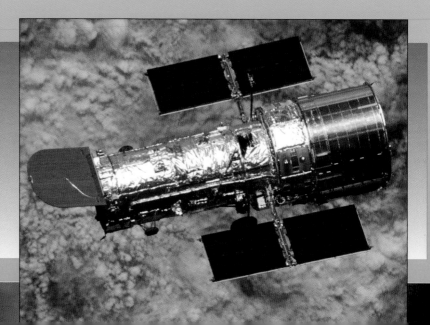

■WHY DOES URANUS ROLL INSTEAD OF SPIN?

Uranus is the only planet that is tilted almost at right angles. Its north and south poles point sideways, rather than from top to bottom.

■ WHAT CAUSED THE POLES OF URANUS TO BE TILTED SO FAR?

We don't know for sure, but the most likely explanation is that in the early days of the solar system, Uranus was knocked sideways by a collision with a planet-sized space object. Calculations show that the impact must have been with something about the size of Earth.

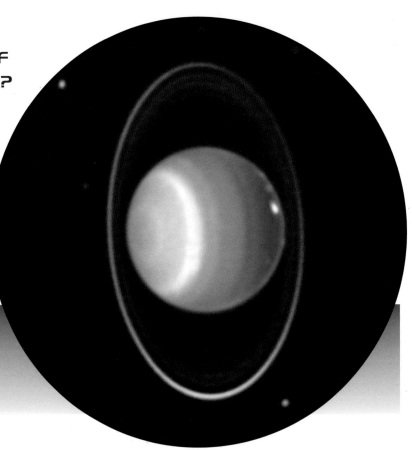

■ For much of the time, viewing Uranus from Earth is like looking at a big target, with the rings circling it like a number of giant hoops.

■ DOES URANUS HAVE A MAGNETIC FIELD?

Yes. Like other gas giants, Uranus has a magnetic field. These are created by powerful electric currents deep inside the mantle. For unknown reasons, magnetism on Uranus is unlike Earth. On Earth, a compass pointing to "magnetic north" points where you would expect it to point: toward the North Pole. The magnetic field of Uranus points sideways, at an angle of nearly 60 degrees.

An oddly-angled magnetic field is something that Uranus shares with Neptune. Neptune has one pointing sideways, at 47 degrees.

WOW!
The **gravity** pull on Uranus is 0.87 times the strength we feel on Earth. A 100 lb (43.5 kg) object on Earth would weigh 87 lb (39.5 kg) on Uranus.

■ WHAT IS THE AXIAL TILT OF A PLANET?

A planet turns like a spinning top, around an imaginary line called its axis. At the ends of the axis are the north and south poles. The angle of the north-south axis is called the **axial tilt**. In the solar system, these vary from the near-vertical angle of Mercury, to the 98-degree sideways roll of Uranus.

▢ Each planet has a slightly different axial tilt. The most tilted planet is Uranus.

1 Mercury	5 Jupiter
2 Venus	6 Saturn
3 Earth	7 Uranus
4 Mars	8 Neptune

HOW MANY RINGS DOES URANUS HAVE?

It has 13 known rings. Unlike Saturn's bright ring system, the rings of Uranus are faint and made mostly of very dark materials.

■ One of the moons that help keep ring particles in place. This view shows some of the inner rings. They are made mostly of small pebbles and rocks.

■ WHAT ARE THE RINGS MADE OF?

Eleven of the rings are made of rocky particles up to about 30 ft (9 m) across. Two rings are made mostly of dust, and there are also some dusty bands between rings.

WOW!
William Herschel thought he saw rings in 1789. The official discovery was by two U.S. astronomers, in 1977. Voyager 2 took the first close-up pictures, in 1986.

■ WHY AREN'T THE RINGS AS BRIGHT AS SATURN'S?

They orbit within the magnetic field of Uranus. Over time, the ring particles have darkened. Today, the rings reflect only about five percent of the Sun's light.

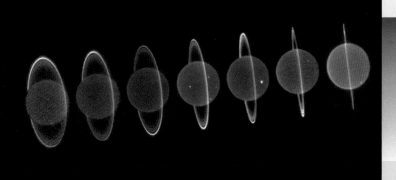

■ Our view of the rings changes as Uranus travels in its 84-year long orbit.
These pictures were taken at annual intervals, starting in 2001. By 2007, the rings could be seen only as a fine line dividing Uranus in two.

■ WHERE DID THE RINGS COME FROM IN THE FIRST PLACE?

Like other rings in the solar system, it is likely the rings of Uranus were formed from the remains of colliding space objects. This happened not long after the planet formed. It is thought that several small moons, breaking up at intervals over the last 4.5 billion years, made what we see today.

■ WHAT KEEPS THEM IN PLACE?

One or more things are at work to keep them in place. Otherwise the rings would spread out and disappear in only a million or so years. One of those "things" is a number of small, **"shepherd" moons**, which orbit near or inside various rings. The moons' gravity pull, although slight, is enough to keep ring particles in place as they whirl around Uranus.

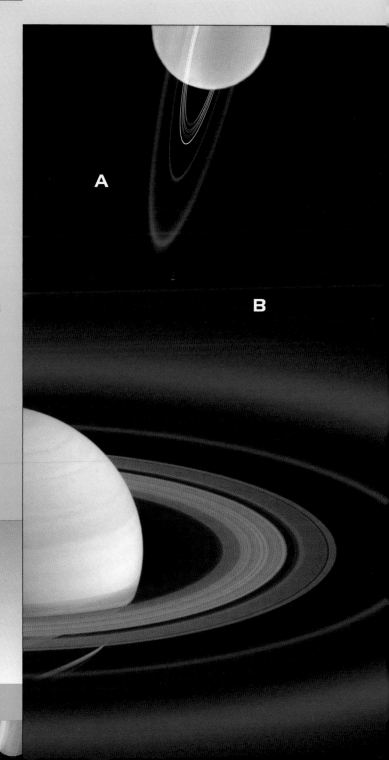

The rings of Uranus (A), compared with the much bigger rings of Saturn (B).
The inner rings of Uranus are mostly a dull gray. Outside these is a red ring and an outer, blue one. They are not really brightly colored like this. The picture has been enhanced to show the differences clearly.

■HOW WARM IS A SUMMER DAY ON URANUS?

The question here could just as easily be "how cold"?
At -364°F (-220°C), Uranus has the chilliest atmosphere in the solar system.

■ The left-hand picture shows how Uranus looks to human eyes, as a plain, pale blue ball. Special filters (right) can reveal faint clouds, with haze over the South Pole.

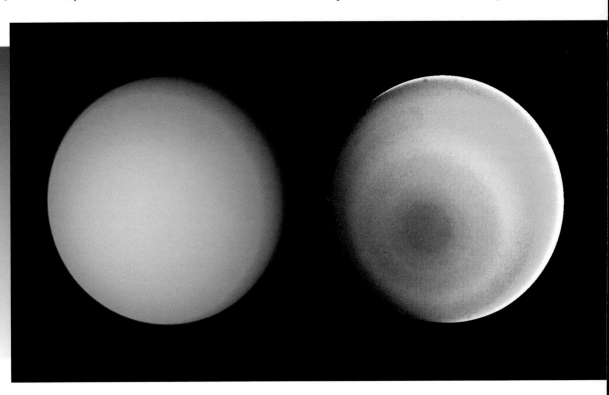

■ WHY IS URANUS SO COLD?

Uranus is a long way from the Sun, so it has to be very cold. The other gas giants have cores that are much hotter, and they give off more heat than they get from the Sun. Uranus does not do this, and we do not know why. One theory is that the collision that knocked Uranus sideways caused some of its heat to gush into space. Another idea is that there may be a hidden layer that stops heat from reaching the surface.

WOW!
Uranus spins faster than the Earth, although not as quickly as the megaplanets, Jupiter and Saturn. It rotates once every 17 hours 14 minutes.

■ ARE THERE STORMS AND CLOUDS ON URANUS?

There are, but nothing like those on the other gas giants. Voyager 2 recorded just ten clouds. Observations since then have shown clouds that have lasted just a few hours. Others have stayed for years at a time.

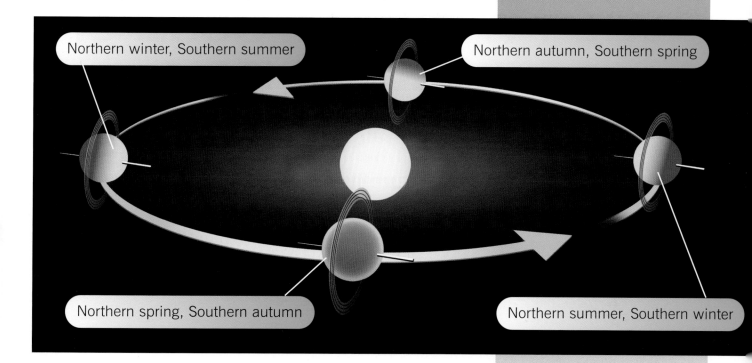

Northern winter, Southern summer

Northern autumn, Southern spring

Northern spring, Southern autumn

Northern summer, Southern winter

■ IS URANUS A WINDY WORLD?

The winds on Uranus vary, depending on where they are. Near the equator, they can blow at more than 220 mph (354 km/h). They move in the opposite direction to Uranus' rotation. Just why this should be, we do not know yet. Closer to the poles, winds gradually reverse, to blow "with" the planet. Speeds of more than 530 mph (853 km/h) have been recorded.

■ Uranus "rolls" along in its orbit, so each pole spends many years in continuous sunlight or darkness.

There is little or no difference in temperature between the two halves of the planet.

■ Here are the planets' average temperatures. Some have more extremes than others. The planets get cooler with their distance from the Sun. Uranus is unusual. It is colder than its neighbor, the furthest planet, Neptune.

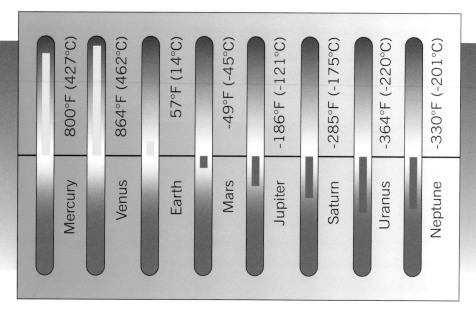

Mercury	Venus	Earth	Mars	Jupiter	Saturn	Uranus	Neptune
800°F (427°C)	864°F (462°C)	57°F (14°C)	-49°F (-45°C)	-186°F (-121°C)	-285°F (-175°C)	-364°F (-220°C)	-330°F (-201°C)

WHAT ARE THE MOONS OF URANUS LIKE?

Uranus has 27 known moons, though only five of them are spheres, like our own Moon. The others are far smaller, boulder-like chunks of rock.

WHAT ARE THE MOONS MADE OF?

The five biggest moons seem to be made of equal mixtures of ice and rock. Different kinds of ice include frozen ammonia and carbon dioxide. The moons are so cold that these materials are every bit as hard as the rocks.

1   2   3   4   5

■ The five biggest moons of Uranus are: Miranda (1), Ariel (2), Umbriel (3), Oberon (4) and Titania (5). Even Titania is only 980 miles (1578 km) across, less than half as big as the Earth's own Moon.

WHAT ABOUT THE SMALLER MOONS?

Other moons include the shepherd moons Cordelia and Ophelia, which keep the edges of the outermost ring neat and tidy. Eight smaller moons orbit in a region so crowded that it is not clear yet why they have not collided with each other. All of these moons are tiny. It is likely that there are more yet to be discovered.

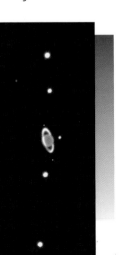

■ William Herschel's discovery of Uranus in 1781 also included two of its biggest moons, Titania and Oberon. It was not until 1948 that the smallest big moon was discovered. U.S. astronomer Gerard Kuiper spotted Miranda. Spotting smaller moons from Earth is difficult. They can be as small as 8 miles (13 km) across.

WHAT COLOR ARE ALL THESE MOONS?

They all come in shades of gray. They are very dark, too. They reflect less than one percent of the light that falls on them.

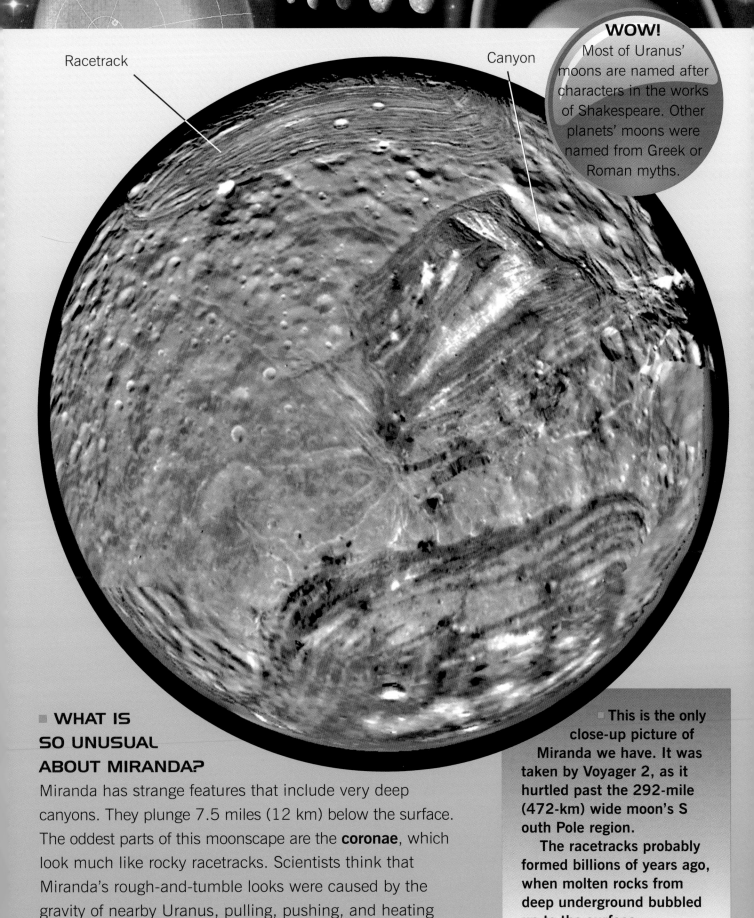

Racetrack

Canyon

■ WHAT IS SO UNUSUAL ABOUT MIRANDA?

Miranda has strange features that include very deep canyons. They plunge 7.5 miles (12 km) below the surface. The oddest parts of this moonscape are the **coronae**, which look much like rocky racetracks. Scientists think that Miranda's rough-and-tumble looks were caused by the gravity of nearby Uranus, pulling, pushing, and heating the ice and rocks that make up the little moon.

□ **This is the only close-up picture of Miranda we have. It was taken by Voyager 2, as it hurtled past the 292-mile (472-km) wide moon's S outh Pole region.**

The racetracks probably formed billions of years ago, when molten rocks from deep underground bubbled up to the surface.

■ HOW LONG IS A YEAR ON NEPTUNE?

At just over 30 AU from the Sun, Neptune's orbital path is a very long one. Neptune takes almost 165 Earth years to complete a single orbit.

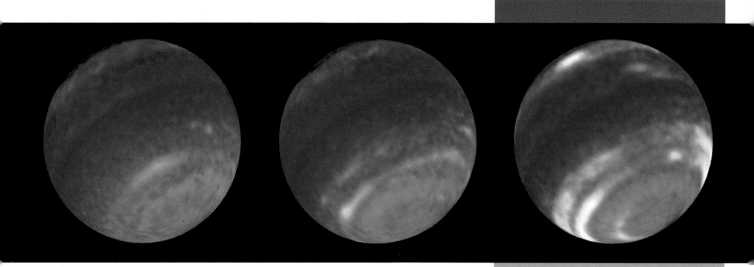

■ HOW LONG ARE THE SEASONS ON NEPTUNE?

Neptune takes 165 Earth years to complete an orbit around the Sun. Its seasons are each about one-quarter of this. Clouds form during Neptune's 41-year summers, probably because of the small amount of extra energy from the distant Sun. Neptune gets 900 times less sunlight than we do, so even daytimes are no brighter than the gentle light of an early evening on Earth.

■ These pictures were taken by the Hubble Space Telescope at two-year intervals, between 1998 and 2002, when the South Pole was starting its summer.

The clouds around the Sun-facing pole slowly get brighter, as the Sun-facing summer pole warms up.

WOW!
One strange effect of Neptune's long summers is that methane gas in the atmosphere warms up just enough to drift up into space from the sunniest polar zone.

■ WHY IS NEPTUNE HOTTER THAN URANUS?

Despite being the outermost planet, Neptune's cloud tops are warmer than those of Uranus. Some heat from Neptune's hotter core must escape to the surface. The planet gives off more than double the heat it receives from the Sun. Some scientists also suggest that heat may be given off when methane clouds break up in the upper atmosphere.

■ HOW FAST DOES NEPTUNE ROTATE?

Like the other gas giants, Neptune has no solid surface, and this allows it to have "**differential rotation**." This means that different parts of the planet turn at different speeds. Neptune has the biggest speed difference of all four gas giants. At its **equator**, Neptune rotates in about 18 hours. Near the poles it whirls around once every 12 hours.

□ Scientists can study Neptune through telescopes, but to get detailed information, we need to send another spacecraft. There are none scheduled to go, but studies have been made for such a mission. This design is from the aerospace company Boeing. The craft is releasing one probe toward Neptune (middle), while another probe (bottom) takes a close look at Triton.

WHAT ARE THE GREAT DARK SPOTS?

The Great Dark Spot was a huge storm, photographed by Voyager 2 in 1989. Since then, similar but smaller spots have appeared.

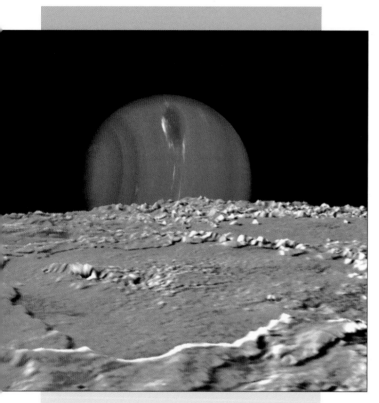

■ **The Great Dark Spot, viewed from just above Neptune's largest moon, Triton. Like the moon Galatea, Triton may one day crash into Neptune, or break up to form a new ring.**

■ HOW LARGE WAS THE SPOT?

The Great Dark Spot (GDS) was about 8,000 miles (13,000 km) wide. That is about the same as Earth. The storm looked much like a smaller version of Jupiter's Great Red Spot. That storm has lasted more than 300 years. The GDS did not last anything as long as this. By 1994, it had disappeared.

■ ARE THERE OTHER SPOTS?

Yes. Neptune has plenty of them. So far none have been as big as the GDS. They include one named "Scooter" because of its speed, and another called the Northern GDS. The spots seem to be spirals of cloud, similar to hurricanes on Earth. The spots are probably made up mostly of methane gas.

WOW!
Neptune's storms and winds are thought to be powered by the heat coming from its core. The rising heat causes huge columns of rising and falling air currents.

■ HOW FAST ARE NEPTUNE'S WINDS?

Neptune is the windiest planet in the solar system, with gales that roar along at up to 1,300 mph (2,100 km/h)! Most winds are slower than this, with speeds of 250 mph (400 km/h) being more usual around Neptune's equator. Like the winds of Uranus, winds on Neptune mostly blow against its rotation near the equator, and with it closer to the poles.

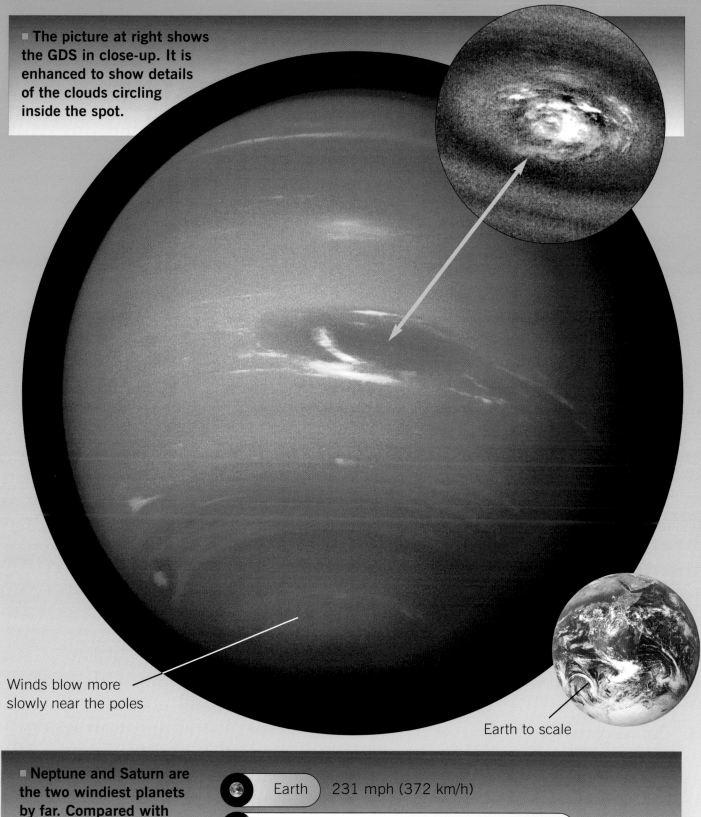

■ The picture at right shows the GDS in close-up. It is enhanced to show details of the clouds circling inside the spot.

Winds blow more slowly near the poles

Earth to scale

■ Neptune and Saturn are the two windiest planets by far. Compared with their wind speeds, even Earth's most violent hurricanes blow at little more than a snail's pace.

Earth   231 mph (372 km/h)

Saturn 1,056 mph (1,700 km/h)

Neptune 1,300 mph (2,100 km/h)

HOW FAINT ARE THE RINGS OF NEPTUNE?

Neptune has seven known rings. They are so faint that they look almost invisible. What we know about them comes from pictures taken by Voyager 2.

WHAT DO THE RINGS LOOK LIKE?

Neptune's rings vary in width, from thin and narrow to broad and wide. They are all very dusty. They are made of countless particles smaller than grains of sand.

The grayish dust means Neptune's rings are dull and dim. This differs from Saturn's rings, which are made mostly of water-ice chunks. Saturn's rings sparkle and gleam as they reflect the Sun's rays.

■ The rings can hardly be seen at all. In this Voyager image, they are shown much brighter than they really are.

■ The five ring arcs are found only in the Adams ring. They change in size and brightness over the years.

WOW!
The gravity pull on Neptune is 1.14 times the strength we feel on the Earth. A 100 lb (43.5 kg) object on Earth would weigh 114 lb (51.7 kg) on Neptune.

WHAT ARE RING ARCS, AND WHY DO THEY EXIST?

They are the brightest parts of the outermost ring, called the Adams ring. It is likely that the brightness is caused not by different kinds of dust particles, but because they are clumped together more thickly. This way, they reflect the dim sunlight better. The reason for the arcs' existence was a mystery to astronomers, until they realized that the gravity of a nearby moon could be moving particles into the arc regions.

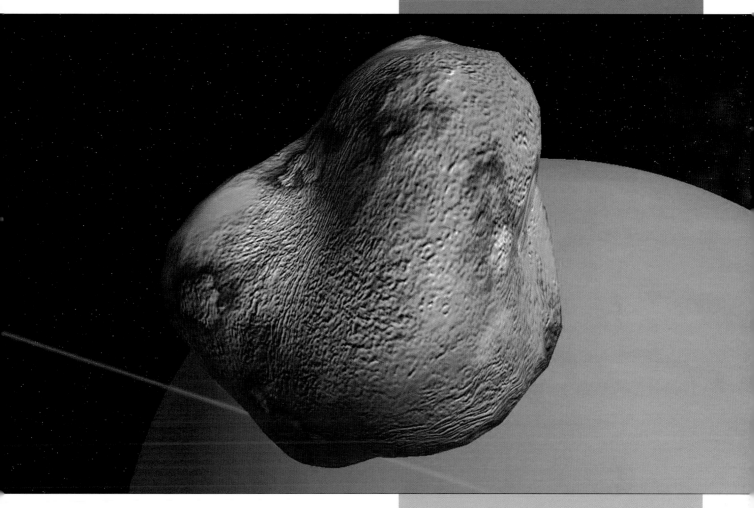

■ WHAT IS GALATEA ?

It is one of Neptune's smallest moons, and is barely 110 miles (180 km) long. Galatea was the key to solving the mystery of the ring arcs. It is thought to be a shepherd moon for the arcs of the Adams ring. Its slight gravity pull is just enough to shuffle dust particles around.

■ ARE NEPTUNE'S RINGS A PERMANENT FEATURE?

The ring particles seem to be in constant motion. Those forming the ring arcs seem even faster. Some of the arcs could be gone by the year 2100, but the main rings are likely to exist for billions of years.

■ Galatea orbits Neptune 620 miles (1,000 km) inside the Adams ring. This distance puts the little moon in great danger. If it spirals much closer to Neptune, it will move inside the Roche Limit. This is a point near a planet where its gravity forces become strong enough to rip a moon apart.

One day, Galatea will do one of two things: it will either fall out of orbit and smash into Neptune or, it will break up into rubble, and form another ring.

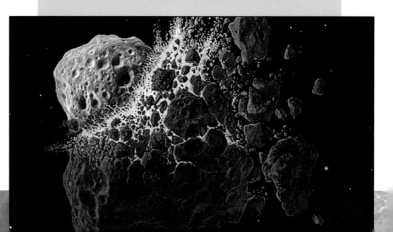

WHAT IS THE BIGGEST MOON OF NEPTUNE?

It is an icy planet-like object called Triton. It is almost as massive as Neptune's dozen other moons and all the rings put together.

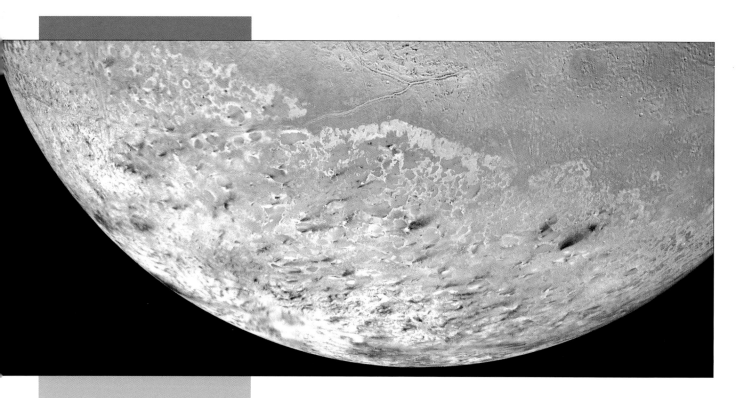

■ Triton measures 841 miles (1,354 km) across, or about three-quarters the size of Earth's Moon. It is a very cold moon, with a surface temperature that is about -391°F (-235°C).

■ WHAT IS TRITON LIKE?

It is very different from Neptune, with icecaps of rock-hard frozen nitrogen, over a core of rock, metals, and water-ice. Triton is an active moon. It has **geysers**, which erupt plumes of nitrogen gas. On page 1, you can see how such a geyser may look.

■ WHAT ABOUT THE OTHER MOONS OF NEPTUNE?

The second biggest moon is called Nereid, but it is just 211 miles (340 km) across. Other moons range in size down to tiny Psamathe. It is a chunk of space rock just 17.4 miles (28 km) long. More tiny moons are likely to be found by future space probes.

WOW!
Triton's geysers are powered by the Sun, which slightly warms some ice under the **crust**, turning it to gas. Then trapped gases explode through the frozen crust.

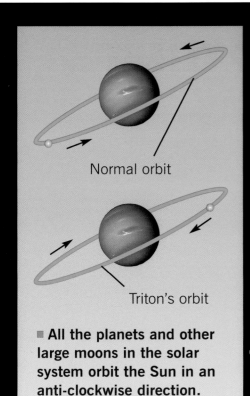

Normal orbit

Triton's orbit

■ All the planets and other large moons in the solar system orbit the Sun in an anti-clockwise direction.

Triton moves the opposite way in a process called retrograde direction. Until it orbited Neptune, Triton may have been a wandering dwarf planet.

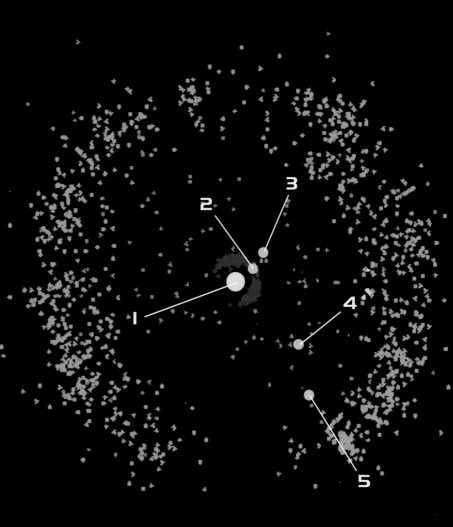

■ WHAT'S STRANGE ABOUT THE DIRECTION OF TRITON'S ORBIT?

Triton moves in the opposite direction to the other large moons in the solar system. This is so unusual that it is likely Triton did not form near Neptune. Instead, it was probably once a **Kuiper Belt** Object (KBO). The Kuiper Belt lies far beyond the planets, in the darkness of the solar system's outer edges.

■ The Kuiper Belt is a huge region that lies beyond the planets. On this computerized diagram, green dots mark some of the biggest KBOs. Also shown are the Sun (1), Jupiter (2), Saturn (3), Uranus (4), and Neptune (5). The Earth and other inner planets are too small to show at this scale.

Triton could have drifted for millions of years in the Kuiper Belt, then moved slowly toward the Sun. Eventually, it passed Neptune, where it was captured by the windy planet's strong gravity. Then Triton went into the orbital path we can see today.

■HOW CAN I OBSERVE URANUS AND NEPTUNE?

Uranus is only just bright enough to be seen faintly by the naked eye. To observe far-off Neptune, you need a powerful telescope.

■ WHAT EQUIPMENT DO ASTRONOMERS USE?

There are many observatories around the world, but the two biggest telescopes are at the Keck Observatory at the summit of the 13,796 (4205 m) high Mauna Kea volcano, in Hawaii. Here, 300-ton (272-tonne) telescopes peer into space. The skies around the observatory are mostly clear and calm. They are far away from any smoke or pollution from towns and cities.

■ HOW DO THE TELESCOPES WORK?

Each telescope has a 33-foot (10-meter) wide mirror, which collects the faint light from distant stars and planets. The mirrors are made of 36 sections that are adjusted constantly by a computer system. This precise equipment gives pictures that are up to ten times sharper than any other ground-based telescope.

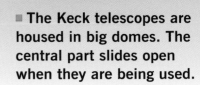

■ **The Keck telescopes are housed in big domes. The central part slides open when they are being used.**

■ **One of the 36 sections that form the telescope mirrors at the Keck Observatory. Before the section is ready to be used, it will be sprayed with a perfect mirror-finish, made of an extremely thin layer of aluminum.**

■ WHY ARE THERE TWO TELESCOPES?

Computers enable the view from two instruments to be combined into one, which gives far better results than would be possible from a single telescope.

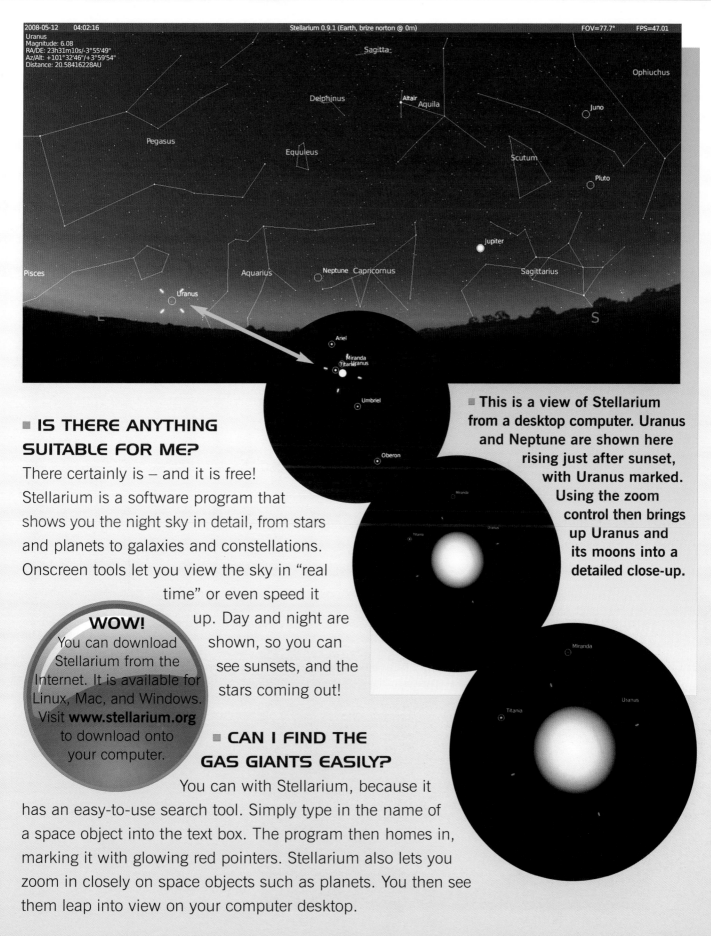

2008-05-12   04:02:16
Uranus
Magnitude: 6.08
RA/DE: 23h31m10s/-3°55'49"
Az/Alt: +101°32'46"/+3°59'54"
Distance: 20.58416228AU

Stellarium 0.9.1 (Earth, brize norton @ 0m)

FOV=77.7°   FPS=47.01

Sagitta

Ophiuchus

Delphinus

Altair
Aquila

Juno

Pegasus

Equuleus

Scutum

Pluto

Jupiter

Pisces

Aquarius

Neptune Capricornus

Sagittarius

S

Uranus

Ariel

Miranda
Titania Uranus

Umbriel

Oberon

Miranda

Titania

Uranus

Miranda

Titania

Uranus

■ IS THERE ANYTHING SUITABLE FOR ME?

There certainly is – and it is free! Stellarium is a software program that shows you the night sky in detail, from stars and planets to galaxies and constellations. Onscreen tools let you view the sky in "real time" or even speed it up. Day and night are shown, so you can see sunsets, and the stars coming out!

WOW!

You can download Stellarium from the Internet. It is available for Linux, Mac, and Windows. Visit **www.stellarium.org** to download onto your computer.

■ CAN I FIND THE GAS GIANTS EASILY?

You can with Stellarium, because it has an easy-to-use search tool. Simply type in the name of a space object into the text box. The program then homes in, marking it with glowing red pointers. Stellarium also lets you zoom in closely on space objects such as planets. You then see them leap into view on your computer desktop.

■ This is a view of Stellarium from a desktop computer. Uranus and Neptune are shown here rising just after sunset, with Uranus marked. Using the zoom control then brings up Uranus and its moons into a detailed close-up.

■ FACTS AND FIGURES

■ URANUS STATISTICS

Diameter

31,765 miles (51,120 km), making Uranus the third biggest planet in the solar system, after Jupiter (the biggest), and Saturn.

Time to rotate ("day")

Uranus turns on average once every 17 hours and 14 minutes.

Time to orbit once around the Sun ("year")

Uranus completes one orbit of the Sun every 84.3 Earth years.

Distance to the Sun

About 1.86 billion miles (3 billion km), some 19.2 AU average.

Composition

Uranus is thought to have a rocky core, surrounded by a fluid mantle made largely of water and ammonia. The outer layers are hydrogen and helium gases.

Temperature

Across the planet, temperatures at the cloud tops average about -364°F (-220°C).

Surface gravity

Here on Earth we live under a force of one gravity, or 1G. Despite its bigger size, Uranus is made of lighter materials, and has a gravity pull of just 0.87G.

Atmosphere

Uranus's atmosphere is made up of about 80 percent hydrogen, 15 percent helium, two percent methane, and traces of other gases.

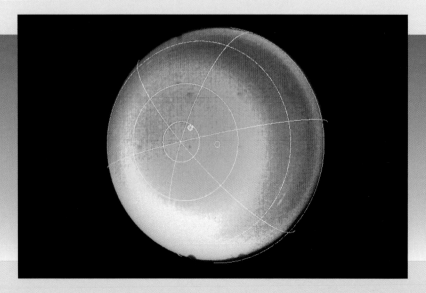

■ The southern half of Uranus is divided into two parts. There is a bright polar cap, with darker clouds circling the planet nearer the equator. A narrow band of cloud between them is called the collar. Both cap and collar are thought to be regions filled with thick methane gas clouds.

■ NEPTUNE STATISTICS

Diameter

At 30,775 miles (49,528 km) across, Neptune is the solar system's fourth largest planet.

Time to rotate ("day")

Neptune turns once every 16 hours and six minutes, on average.

Time to orbit once around the Sun ("year")

Neptune completes one orbit of the Sun every 164.8 Earth years.

Distance to the Sun

About 2.83 billion miles (4.55 billion km), or 30.1 AU average.

Composition

Neptune is thought to be similar to Uranus, with a rocky core. The mantle is rich in water and ammonia, known to astronomers as "ices."

Temperature

Temperatures at the top of Neptune's clouds are about -330°F (-201°C).

Surface gravity

About 1.14 times Earth's gravity.

Atmosphere

Neptune's atmosphere is about 80 percent hydrogen and 18 percent helium, 1.5 percent methane, and traces of other gases.

■ This is the sort of view you might see from Neptune's cloud tops.

The distant Sun is tinted bluish-white by the mixture of gases in the atmosphere, and it gives very little heat.

For humans, Neptune is a deadly place. The air is made of poison gases. It is so cold that you would freeze solid in less than a minute.

■GLOSSARY

Here are explanations for many of the terms used in this book.

Ammonia A colorless gas with a very strong smell. It can be dissolved in water to be used as a cleaning fluid. On the gas giants, it is found in their atmospheres.

Atmosphere The layers of gases surrounding most of the planets.

■ Scientists who made early gas giant discoveries include William Herschel (left) and Urbain Le Verrier (right).

AU Astronomical Unit, the average distance from Earth to the Sun is 93 million miles (150 million km). The AU is used as a measure for big distances in space.

Axial tilt The angle at which a planet leans as it spins around. Earth has a tilt of 23.5 degrees, Neptune 28.3 degrees, but Uranus leans sideways, at 97.8 degrees.

Core The center of a planet. The cores of Uranus and Neptune are both thought to be very hot.

Coronae Strange, racetrack markings found on Neptune's moon, Triton.

Crust The hard, surface layer of many planets, or a moon such as Triton.

Differential rotation The way in which a gas giant may have various parts rotating at different speeds, unlike a solid planet like Earth.

Equator The imaginary band around the waist of a planet, dividing it into northern and southern halves, or hemispheres.

Gas giant A large planet made mostly of gases, with no solid surface. Uranus and Neptune are gas giants, as are Jupiter and Saturn. Rocky worlds and moons have a hard crust that you could walk on.

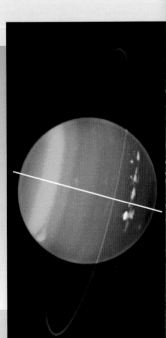

■ **This view of Uranus, taken at Hawaii's Keck Observatory, shows its extreme axial tilt (white line). The ring is enhanced to show it clearly. It's not as bright as this in real life.**

Part of the Sun to the same scale as the planets

1 2 3 4 5 6 7 8

Geyser On Triton, a plume of cold gas sprayed from under the ground.

Gravity The universal force of attraction between all objects.

Helium The second most common element in the universe.

Hydrogen The most common element in the universe.

Ice giant, ices A planet that contains "ices" in its interior. These ices are substances with low boiling points.

Kuiper Belt The vast halo of space objects that circles the Sun, far beyond the planets.

Magnetic field The area of influence around anything that has magnetism.

Mantle The hot, fluid part of a gas giant surrounding the core.

Methane A colorless, flammable gas. On Earth it is the main part of natural gas, used for heating homes.

Orbit The curving path a space object takes around a more massive one, such as a planet orbiting the Sun, or a moon moving around a planet.

Retrograde A space object that has a rotation, or orbit, in the reverse direction to normal.

Shepherd moon A moon that orbits near a ring system. Its gravity keeps particles in place in the ring.

Solar system The name for the Sun and the eight major planets, and other space objects that circle it.

■ Here are the Sun and major planets:
1 Mercury
2 Venus
3 Earth
4 Mars
5 Jupiter
6 Saturn
7 Uranus
8 Neptune

■ GOING FURTHER

Using the Internet is a great way to expand your knowledge of the gas giants.

Your first visit should be to the site of the U.S. space agency, NASA. Its site shows almost everything to do with space, from the history of spaceflight and astronomy, and plans for future space missions.

There are also websites that give detailed space information. Try these sites to start with:

http://www.nasa.gov — The biggest space site.
http://www.space.com — Lots of general interest.
http://voyager.jpl.nasa.gov/ — The Voyager website.
http://www.ifa.hawaii.edu/faculty/jewitt/kb.html — Info on the Kuiper Belt.

■INDEX